WET WEATHER COVER

Oliver Cotton

WET WEATHER COVER

OBERON BOOKS
LONDON

Published in 2010 by Oberon Books Ltd
Electronic edition published in 2012

Oberon Books Ltd
521 Caledonian Road, London N7 9RH
Tel: 020 7607 3637 / Fax: 020 7607 3629
e-mail: info@oberonbooks.com
www.oberonbooks.com

A catalogue record for this book is available from the British Library.

PB ISBN: 978-1-84002-996-3
E ISBN: 978-1-84943-885-8

Cover photo by Stephen Bush. Logo design by Pete le May.

eBook conversion by Replika Press PVT Ltd, India.

Visit www.oberonbooks.com to read more about all our books and to buy them. You will also find features, author interviews and news of any author events, and you can sign up for e-newsletters so that you're always first to hear about our new releases.

Wet Weather Cover was first performed at the Tiffany Theatre, Los Angeles on 24 June 1999.

This new version received its UK premiere at the King's Head Theatre on 20 January 2010, with the following cast (in order of appearance):

BRAD Michael Brandon
PEPE Pepe Balderrama
STUART Steve Furst

Director Kate Fahy
Designer Tanya McCallin
Lighting Designer Emma Chapman
Sound Designer Tim Middleton

Characters

BRAD
An American actor in his mid-forties. Heavy
build. Italian looks.

STUART
An English actor in his forties.

PEPE
A Spanish man in his forties. Small. Neat.
Speaks no English.

SCENE ONE

Somewhere in central Spain. Morning. Nine a.m. A trailer is parked on some wasteland at the base of a mountain. It is raining heavily.

BRAD is sprawled on a seat at the rear section of the trailer. He is wearing sixteenth century costume – shirt, leather breeches and boots – and he is half hidden from view by a table. On the table are a walkie-talkie radio and a script. Also various paper cups etc.

> *The walkie-talkie splutters into life over massive interference. The voice at the other end is indecipherable. BRAD reaches lazily for the walkie-talkie and clicks down the button.*

> *Indecipherable, ear-splitting splutter.*

BRAD: Well how the fuck do you think I'm doing Chris?

> *Indecipherable, ear-splitting splutter.*

What? I can't hear you.

> *Indecipherable, ear-splitting splutter.*

No. I'll go to make up when I know they're going to use me.

> *Indecipherable, ear-splitting splutter.*

Aha – what scene?

> *Indecipherable, ear-splitting splutter. BRAD looks out of the window.*

98A? It's pouring with fucking rain!

> *Indecipherable, ear-splitting splutter.*

Listen – I want to know why I was called –

> *Indecipherable, ear-splitting splutter.*

Jesus! I said I want to know why I was called at 5.30 in the fucking morning. I've been sitting here for the last two hours. This stupid thing doesn't work and even if it did there's no point because you never pick up! My cell has no

7

signal, the trailer leaks, no one's been near! What the fuck Chris!

Indecipherable, ear-splitting splutter. BRAD shakes his head in frustration. He leafs through his script.

Breakfast? Yeah. I had some freezing tortilla round six. 98A's the fort stuff right?

Indecipherable, ear-splitting splutter.

So that's everyone isn't it?

Indecipherable, ear-splitting splutter.

Aha. When were they called?

Indecipherable, ear-splitting splutter.

Listen Chris – it's an hour and a half's drive from the hotel ok?

The door of the trailer opens and a smallish man enters. He is carrying an armful of leather jerkins and a breastplate. This is PEPE, the dresser. He speaks no English – but curses continually in Spanish. PEPE starts to hang the costume in the narrow wardrobe.

Indecipherable, ear-splitting splutter.

So it makes a difference if they left five minutes ago or an hour ago. Right?

Indecipherable, ear-splitting splutter.

What I'm saying is there's no point in going to make up till I know I'm going to be used. It only takes ten minutes.

A silence.

What I want to know is what happened to twenty-seven? Chris? I was called at five thirty this morning to do twenty-seven. What happened to it?

Silence.

Chris? Chris?

The line has gone dead. He puts the walkie-talkie down and falls back onto the seat.

PEPE: Es Impossible de encontrar tu camisa gris. Le he preguntado a Dora y me ha dicho que esta aqui pero no la veo en nigun lado.

BRAD speaks no Spanish and is unresponsive.

No lleva la camisa correcta. Me escucha? Tengo que llevar esta a Dora. Brad?

PEPE goes over to BRAD and gestures towards his shirt.

Mira Dame esta camisa y yo te doy una camiseta hasta que encuentres la camisa gris.

A beat.

BRAD: What do you want?

PEPE: Por favor dame tu camisa. No es la correcta.

BRAD: That's right. This is my shirt.

PEPE: Brad esta no es la camisa correcta. En la noventa y ocho tu lleva la gris.

He gestures for BRAD to take it off.

BRAD: No – no.

PEPE: Si – si! La ostia! Escuchame! Esta camisa es encorrecta. Yo que se, quizas Romero tiene la gris, le voy a preguntar.

BRAD: Shall I tell you something about your friend Romero?

PEPE: Romero si.

BRAD: Romero si – he's a stupid, brainless, half-assed pimp who wouldn't know a shirt from a fucking dress. You understand?

PEPE: Si creo que Romero tiene la camisa.

BRAD: Romero what? I can't understand what you're saying for Christ's sake. This is my shirt. I've been wearing it since seven o'clock this morning.

PEPE: Joder! Dame la camisa Brad. Aqui tengo una camisetta para ti.

PEPE holds up the vest.

BRAD: I don't want that. I can't do the scene in that. I want my shirt.

PEPE: Por el amor dios Brad! Romero tiene tu camisa. Entiende me!

BRAD: Wait a minute – where is Romero?

PEPE looks puzzled.

Where – is – Romero? Donde Romero?

PEPE: Ah! Set.

BRAD: Ok wait.

BRAD clicks the switch on the walkie-talkie.

Chris? This is Brad. Chris?

Silence.

Chris? Somebody for Christ's sake. Is somebody there?!

The door swings open fast and STUART struggles into the trailer. He has been running through the rain and carries a small rucksack in one hand and a plate in the other. On the plate is a bacon roll wrapped in wet tinfoil and a carefully balanced coffee cup. STUART is half-dressed in his costume over which he wears an anorak. His head is covered with a transparent plastic hood to keep the rain off his wig. As he moves gingerly into the trailer his hand shakes and he spills half of his coffee on the floor.

STUART: Shit!

STUART puts the other things down and takes some tissues from the sideboard. He bends down and starts to mop up the coffee.

Why doesn't someone put some boards out there?

BRAD continues to try to make contact with the set.

BRAD: Hullo – hullo. Chris? Steve? Brian? Anybody?

PEPE: Llevo media hora dicendole! Romero tiene su camisa!

BRAD: Tell him to calm down will you.

STUART: He says Romero has your shirt.

BRAD: Jesus!

PEPE: El debe estar llevando la camisa gris

STUART: Apparently you should be wearing the grey shirt.

BRAD: The grey shirt? Why?

PEPE: Mire…Dora dice que el debe llevar la camisa gris en la escena noventa ocho

STUART: Dora says you're supposed to wear the grey shirt in scene 98.

BRAD: Listen – when his faggot friend Romero the fucking gypsy gets down here with my grey shirt I'll put it on. Till then I'm staying like I am.

The walkie-talkie suddenly comes to life and Chris's voice crackles over. Indecipherable, ear-splitting splutter. BRAD clicks the switch.

BRAD: I've been trying to reach you. What happened?

Indecipherable, ear-splitting splutter.

BRAD: Yes Stuart's here. Is Romero with you?

Indecipherable, ear-splitting splutter.

BRAD: Ok, when you find him, ask him if he's got my grey shirt for scene 98 will you.

Indecipherable, ear-splitting splutter.

BRAD: Here he is.

BRAD passes the walkie-talkie to STUART, who throws the tissue into a cardboard box and wearily takes the handset.

BRAD: You ok? You look terrible.

STUART: Hullo – Chris?

Indecipherable, ear-splitting splutter.

STUART: No, I came down with one of the stunt guys.

BRAD: You must have a death wish.

Indecipherable, ear-splitting splutter.

STUART: I know the bus hadn't arrived at the hotel when we left. That's why I grabbed the lift.

STUART starts to unwrap his bacon roll. Indecipherable, ear-splitting splutter.

STUART: Yeah I've done make up. All ready to go.

BRAD: Could have fooled me.

STUART: It's 98 isn't it?

Indecipherable, ear-splitting splutter.

STUART: Are you shooting anything?

Indecipherable, ear-splitting splutter.

BRAD: Tell him to find Romero.

STUART: Brad says can you find Romero? Hullo? Hullo?

He shrugs and passes the walkie-talkie back to BRAD.

He's gone.

BRAD: Asshole. They're all assholes.

STUART points at the walkie-talkie.

STUART: Why've we got a walkie-talkie in here?

BRAD: They got no runners. Half the crew's down with the bug.

STUART: So we've got to use this all day?

BRAD: What am I? The oracle?

To PEPE.

BRAD: I'm keeping this shirt on till Romero turns up. Ok?

PEPE shrugs and leaves. STUART takes a bite of his roll.

This happened last week. Remember? With my boots?

STUART spits out a piece of bacon fat.

STUART: Ugh!

BRAD: These people don't know what they're doing.

In disgust STUART throws the remainder of the bacon roll into the cardboard box.

BRAD: Who cares what shirt I'm wearing –?

STUART wipes his mouth with his sleeve. He sniffs his hand and his face puckers at the smell. He opens the trailer door.

BRAD: – it's covered with all that leather shit anyway.

STUART starts looking around his end of the trailer.

STUART: There was a tub of wet wipes here yesterday.

BRAD: I ate them.

STUART opens a drawer and rummages through it. He closes the drawer and opens an overhead locker. It's overfull and a lot of things fall out onto the floor. Bits of script, paper cups, a piece of electrical equipment, wire etc. He gazes at it all in exhausted exasperation.

STUART: Jesus!

STUART bends down and starts picking the stuff up. He throws it all into the cardboard box.

BRAD: They just focus on all the wrong things – you know? It's so tedious.

BRAD sticks his leg in the air showing his boot.

I asked them a million times and everyday they say they'll do it and every day it's exactly the same. Why?

STUART finds the tub of wet wipes amongst the rubbish. He wipes the grease from his hands and mouth. BRAD takes the boot off, closes the trailer door and walks over to STUART.

BRAD: Put your hand in this.

STUART puts his hand wearily into the boot.

No. Down at the bottom.

STUART puts his arm down further.

BRAD: Feel it?

STUART: What am I feeling for?

BRAD: There's a nail there Stuart!

STUART feels around inside the boot. BRAD rams his arm down the boot next to STUART's.

There! Give me your hand! Ok – there! Feel it? There!

STUART: I can feel a sort of bump yeah –

BRAD: It's not a bump for Christ's sake – it's a nail! It's killing me when I walk.

STUART takes his arm out.

STUART: You should ask them to fix it.

BRAD: I asked them a million times! I told you.

STUART removes the lid from his coffee cup, sips and winces.

STUART: Christ! Who made this?

He sits down holding his head. BRAD gives the cardboard box a kick.

BRAD: I mean what's all this crap doing here? Most of it's from other productions anyway.

He bends down and picks up a crumpled page of script from the box.

See? This is all in Spanish.

He hands it to STUART who gives it a perfunctory read.

BRAD: What's it say?

STUART translates slowly.

STUART: Juanita and Ramon are in a bar. She's – um – she's –

BRAD: Holding his dick.

BRAD has his hand inside the boot again.

Maybe I could fix this myself.

STUART crumples the page and throws it into the box. BRAD gets up and opens a drawer. He starts to rummage through the stuff in it.

There must be a knife in here somewhere. A screwdriver would do.

He finds a penknife in the drawer.

Great.

BRAD goes back to his end of the trailer. He opens the knife blades one by one trying to work out which one to use. STUART opens the trailer door.

By the way what happened to you last night?

A beat. STUART massages his head.

You disappeared.

STUART: Oh – right. Yeah. I was tired –

BRAD: Aha?

STUART: – and the bar was so full. I –

BRAD: You should have stayed.

STUART: I couldn't take the noise.

BRAD: Great night.

STUART: I could see that. Who was she?

BRAD: Works at the other hotel. Her friend asked after you.

STUART: Really?

BRAD: Yeah. You missed out. You get some sleep?

STUART shakes his head.

STUART: My room's over the bar.

BRAD: Change rooms.

BRAD reaches out and closes the door.

STUART: Why do you keep doing that? It's like an oven in here!

BRAD: I like it warm.

STUART: I'm just trying to get some air Brad.

BRAD: Open the window.

STUART: I've tried – it doesn't work.

BRAD: I had a fever – remember. I need to keep the place at a constant temperature.

STUART: Why?

BRAD: Because I don't want to get sick again Stuart! Okay? I don't want –

STUART: But why can't we have some air –?

A beat.

It's all steamed up.

STUART moves to his end of the trailer and sits down.

It's so smelly.

A beat.

Don't you think it's smelly in here?

STUART gets up. He fiddles with the skylight on the roof. It won't open.

So did you – last night – did you –

BRAD: What?

STUART: Did you – get any sleep?

BRAD: No.

STUART: You mean –

BRAD: I mean I didn't get any sleep. Ok?

> *STUART looks at BRAD who looks back. Eventually STUART nods. He finds a pair of scissors and starts to lever one edge of the skylight upwards.*

STUART: Where were you? In your room?

BRAD: Nope.

STUART: Right.

> *STUART pushes the plastic skylight hard and a stream of water hit's him in the face.*

STUART: Oh Christ!

> *He wipes his eye. BRAD gives him a disdainful look.*

How was it?

BRAD: Great. It was great! Ok? What is this the inquisition?

STUART: Sorry.

BRAD continues to work on the boot. His attention is suddenly taken by a steady drip of water through the skylight. STUART follows his gaze and closes his eyes wearily.

BRAD: Thanks a lot Stuart.

STUART takes one of the plastic cups and puts it under the drip. They watch for a moment as the water hits the cup. Its sound is regular and relentless.

I'm going to enjoy listening to that.

The door opens and PEPE comes in fast.

PEPE: Debo tener su camisa immediamente. Romero no la tiene.

BRAD: What's he saying?

STUART: Give him your shirt Brad.

BRAD: What happened to Romero?

STUART: Romero doesn't have your shirt.

BRAD looks at PEPE.

BRAD: Oh really? Where was Romero? Donde Romero?

PEPE: Romero esta en el lavabo y muy indispuesto. El doctor ya esta en camino.

STUART: Romero's unwell and in the toilet. Apparently the doctor's coming.

BRAD: Great. Maybe the doctor has my shirt.

STUART changes the subject.

STUART: Have you got any paracetamol?

A beat.

Brad, have you got any paracetamol?

BRAD: No.

STUART: Aspirin?

BRAD: I just said – no.

PEPE: Por que se niega el a darme su camisa?!!

STUART: Give him your shirt Brad so he can grey it up.

BRAD: You know what's fucking ridiculous? That this bunch of assholes didn't bring enough shirts. Why is this the only one I can wear? There must be others?

STUART holds his hand to his forehead to try and dull the pain of his headache.

STUART: I don't understand the point you're trying to make. Give him your shirt and he'll take it away and let you have it later. What's the big deal?

BRAD: The big deal Stuart is that I don't like things being inefficient and half-assed. It's not my fault that Romero's sick. It's not my fault they only brought one shirt and lost all the others. It's not my fault that –

STUART: Nobody's saying it's your fault –

BRAD: No. I'm saying it's their fault. Ok? It's their fault and I don't see why I should co-operate with people who can't get their shit together. That's all.

The nail comes through the sole of BRAD's boot.

Oh Christ! Now look what I did!

BRAD throws the boot to one side.

Fuck it!

He gets up, takes the shirt off in one rapid movement and gives it to PEPE. Then he takes off the boot, points to the knife hole and screams.

See?!!

PEPE takes the shirt and moves off.

BRAD: What about the boot? Hey – what about –

But PEPE is gone.

Can you fucking believe that? Asshole!!!

STUART moves up the trailer and lies down on the seat.

BRAD: What time was your call by the way?

STUART: What?

BRAD: What time was your call?

STUART: Seven. We were all called for seven.

BRAD explodes with indignation making STUART jump.

BRAD: WHY FOR CHRIST'S SAKE?!!!!!!!

STUART: Brad please don't shout –

BRAD: WHY?!!

A beat.

I mean there's nothing you could have done! I'm supposed to be doing twenty-seven. Now! You know? Only reason I'm not is because of the rain. But if I was – well it'd have taken a minimum of three hours. I mean it's a long scene. Three or four set ups at least. The ride up, the guy shooting arrows, dismounting, hiding, the fight – I mean it's long. So why were you all called so early?

A beat.

I mean what's the point?! What is the fucking point of dragging you bunch of English fags out here in the pouring, stinking, freezing rain when you could all be whining at each other back at the hotel. It doesn't make any sense. Does it?

STUART: We're wet weather cover aren't we?

BRAD: Oh come on! Don't give me all that weather shit! There isn't any cover! What are they going to do with you guys out here?

STUART takes a deep breath.

STUART: I thought we were doing the fort.

BRAD takes a deep breath.

BRAD: Stuart the fort is all exterior.

STUART: No it's not –

BRAD: Yes it fucking is – it's all exterior. Have you seen it?

STUART: No.

BRAD: I saw it last night.

STUART: Really? How far is it?

BRAD: Halfway up the mountain. About twenty minutes by car.

STUART groans.

It's all in the open. There's nowhere to get shelter.

STUART: Yeah but it's not finished. They've got to put the roof on. I thought that's what they were doing now.

BRAD grabs his script and rifles through the pages to scene 98. He takes it over to where STUART is lying and shows it to him.

BRAD: Look at the script for Christ's sake – it's all in the open! Where does it say we're inside?

STUART looks at the script through one eye.

Where?

STUART: I just presumed the scene was inside.

BRAD stares at him in disbelief.

BRAD: Cortes sits on his horse and talks to his men in a room? Is that what you presumed?

STUART: I didn't read the scene very carefully. I only stand in the background and I don't say anything

BRAD: Like your life right?

STUART: Precisely. Like my life. Thanks Brad.

STUART turns over onto his side and curls up.

BRAD: And on that basis you allowed yourself to be driven here at eighty miles an hour by some drunken, half-asleep dipshit – so you could stand in the background of a scene you didn't read very carefully and not say anything?

STUART: What do you say in it? I can't see any lines for you there. The only person who speaks is Cortes.

BRAD: I'm not here to do that scene Stuart. I'm here to do twenty-seven and if you look at that you'll see that I say quite a bit. Ok?

STUART: But they're not doing twenty-seven Brad! If they were doing twenty-seven what are you doing here with no armour and the wrong shirt on?

BRAD: I've been here since seven Stuart! I was called at five thirty to do twenty seven. Ok?

STUART: What do you want? A medal?

BRAD: It's raining Stuart. Ok? So I can't do my scene. Ok? I can't do my fucking scene because it's FUCKING RAINING! Ok?

A beat.

So all these guys are on their way to do a scene that can't be done. It's pointless.

The water drips relentlessly into the cup.

I can't stand this dripping Stuart. I'm serious now. I mean it's like we have a water clock in here. We have to do something.

STUART lies very still.

BLACKOUT

SCENE TWO

About one hour later.

There is a brief pause between scenes during which the rain can be heard pelting ferociously on the roof. Then a moaning can be heard in the dark. It increases in intensity until it becomes a scream.

Lights up.

> *STUART is sleeping. BRAD is standing under the skylight allowing the water to drip on his head.*

BRAD: Aaaahhhh! I can't stand it! I can't stand it! The endless drip, drip, drip of the water, endlessly dripping on my head. The ghastly rhythm of the infernal drops as they hit the same spot time after time! – again and again and again! I can't bear it anymore Sergeant! It's driving me crazy! Crazy I tell you!

> *STUART stirs and slowly opens his eyes as BRAD rants on.*

BRAD: It's different for you! You're used to it! You and your kind! You're used to water dripping on your head – but I'm different. I can't take it. I thought I was tough but I'm not. I'm just a poor country boy who should never have come out here! I should never have listened to all your fine words! I should have stayed home where I belong with my girl and my folks and my soft toys. Well I'm not going to take it! I'm going to tell them everything! Yes everything – you hear? I'm going to tell them who has the plans and who has the chewing gum and who has the toilet paper! Because I don't care anymore! I don't care! Guards! Guards!

A beat.

Come on Stuart – be a guard or something.

> *STUART lies staring at BRAD through gummed eyes.*

Come on be a guard.

STUART closes his eyes again for a moment. BRAD gives up.

Ok. Fuck you.

BRAD wipes the water from his face. He takes the polystyrene cup, opens the door and empties it.

Fuck you.

BRAD stares out bleakly into the rain before closing the door and replacing the cup under the drip.

STUART: What's happening?

BRAD: Nothing.

BRAD goes to the table and opens a thermos of coffee.

STUART: So why did you wake me?

BRAD: Dora sent some coffee over. You want some?

STUART sighs and sits up.

STUART: Please.

BRAD pours two cups and hands one to STUART.

BRAD: Oh – and I got you some pills.

He gives them to STUART.

STUART: Great. Thanks.

STUART swallows the pills with a swig of coffee and sits with his eyes closed.

BRAD: How's your head?

STUART: A bit better.

A beat.

How long did I sleep?

BRAD: About an hour – maybe more.

STUART sips his coffee. Takes a book from his bag.

BRAD: Did you bring your laptop?

STUART: No.

BRAD: Oh Jesus!

A beat.

What's that?

STUART: Micky lent it to me.

BRAD: Is it the one about Marlowe?

STUART: Aha.

BRAD: Why don't you take that stupid hood off?

STUART feels his head.

You look like my aunt.

STUART laughs.

STUART: I forgot I was wearing it.

He takes the plastic hood off revealing a wig with a shaved tonsure at the crown.

BRAD: One of the reasons I never wear one of those things. I'd rather use a hat or put my script over my head.

STUART: Your aunt wore one of these?

BRAD: Always. Even when it wasn't raining.

STUART: Really? Why?

BRAD: You tell me. Fucking festival of embarrassment!

BRAD goes to the wardrobe and gets out a costume tunic top. He puts it on.

BRAD: I'm getting chilly. How about you?

STUART: Chilly? Chilly! How can you be chilly? It's ten thousand degrees in here!

BRAD: Bullshit! That fever's still lurking. I got to keep myself warm.

STUART: Maybe you've got Malaria.

BRAD looks suddenly concerned.

BRAD: Malaria? Can you get that here?

STUART sips his coffee, half reading.

STUART: Of course.

BRAD: What? In Spain?

STUART: Let's just pray Romero hasn't got it. What jabs did you have?

BRAD: Jabs?

STUART: Yeah. You know –

STUART mimes an injection.

BRAD: Oh shots! The word is 'shots' Stuart.

BRAD looks worried.

I didn't have any shots.

A beat.

STUART: You're kidding?

BRAD: No I'm not. I didn't have any shots. What did you have?

A beat.

STUART: I think you should let the doctor have a look at you Brad. I mean if you've already had a fever and now you're feeling chilly. That's how Romero started.

BRAD: You mean everyone had shots?

STUART: It's EEC regulations.

BRAD: Oh shit! EEC what?

STUART: Didn't you sign the sheet?

BRAD: Sheet?

STUART: The insurance sheet?

BRAD: I never got one!

STUART: That's ridiculous. There's a whole range of listed conditions here. Malaria, Bilharzias, Swamp fever, Cholera, Dysentery, –

BRAD: Jesus!

STUART: Black Jack, Beri-beri, Weil's disease –

BRAD: Weil's disease! What the fuck is Vile's disease?

STUART: I think it's spread by rat's urine.

BRAD: Rat's urine!

STUART: Yeah. Gets in the rain.

BRAD: What? The urine?!!

STUART: That's why I was wearing the hood.

BRAD: But how the fuck does it get in the rain?

STUART: Transpiration.

BRAD: Transpi-what?

STUART: The rats piss on the ground. The piss evaporates, goes up to the sky, comes down in the rain. That's why Spanish men wear hats.

BRAD: Because of the rat's urine?

STUART: It's a well-known fact.

BRAD is really disturbed. STUART is having trouble not laughing.

STUART: Did you get wet this morning?

BRAD: Not really. Just a few drops when I ran from the car but-

BRAD catches him smirking.

What?

A beat.

Oh no! You asshole!

STUART is hysterical.

I really believed you! Shit! I really believed you!

BRAD starts to laugh. STUART opens the door.

Rat's urine! That was good Stuart. You really got me! But what about all the others. Malaria and –

STUART: I made them up! For Christ's sake! We're not in the tropics –

BRAD closes the door with a bang.

or are we? Oh God! What do I have to do to get some air?!!

BRAD: Go outside.

STUART gives up and falls back onto his seat. He fiddles with the plastic hat.

STUART: So – your aunt –

BRAD: Talking of rat's urine.

STUART: Why was she so embarrassing?

BRAD: Who knows? I think it was genetic. Like – you know – some people get too tall, some people have hair lips, some people are left handed – She was congenitally embarrassing. I don't think there was anything she could have done about it. It was a syndrome. Know what I mean?

STUART: Aha. Does it have a name?

BRAD: Yeah, it's called Asshole's Syndrome.

BRAD concentrates on the buttons of his tunic.

The stupid bitch used to stand at the school gates wearing a plastic hood – and grinning like an ape. I mean it was really embarrassing.

STUART: Where was this? LA?

BRAD: No – New York.

He grabs the plastic hood, puts it on his head and imitates her waving and calling.

'Bradly! Bradly! Here I am! Here I am! Wooohooo-Wooohooo' – that's the noise she used to make – 'Wooohooo-Wooohooo'. I used to pray she wouldn't do it but she always did. She always did. And everyone would stare. Oh God! I could see them thinking 'why is that kid being picked up by a baboon?' You know?

STUART: How old were you?

BRAD: Five – six. And then we'd go on the bus – that was the worst. Listening to her talk all sorts of garbage at the top of her horrible voice – all about Jesus and Mary and how she'd met them in the park or something. And everyone would be trying to find somewhere else to sit.

STUART: And this happened every day?

BRAD: It happened every single day of my first year at school. Every single, fucking day.

STUART gets up and takes the plastic hood from BRAD. While BRAD speaks he pushes the skylight open, places the plastic hood in the opening and closes the skylight tightly on top of it.

STUART: What was her name?

BRAD: Celestina.

STUART: Celestina. Nice name.

BRAD: Yeah – she tried to stab her cousin; with his own chisel – thought he was the Anti-Christ!

He looks at his handiwork. The dripping has stopped.

STUART: There you are. A home made gasket. I'm a genius.

BRAD: I'll sort of miss the cup.

STUART resumes his seat and takes a book from his bag.

STUART: Maybe she did meet them.

BRAD: What?

STUART: Maybe she did meet Jesus and Mary.

BRAD goes to the window, rubs the steam off and peers out.

BRAD: We can't shoot in this. It's like a monsoon out there.

STUART: I mean – how frustrating to meet Jesus in the park and nobody believes you.

BRAD: How frustrating to be Jesus and meet her.

STUART laughs and returns to his book.

BRAD: Micky was going to lend me that.

STUART looks up in surprise.

STUART: Really? I didn't know you were –

BRAD: Interested? In Christopher Marlowe and how he died?

STUART: Yeah –

BRAD: I'm not. I don't give a running fuck.

A beat. STUART returns to the book.

That's what you were doing last night isn't it? While we were making out with the Spanish babes, you were in your room reading about a fifteenth century faggot!

STUART: Sixteenth century.

STUART reads. BRAD stretches. STUART reads. BRAD drums with a knife. STUART reads. BRAD opens the wardrobe and stares. He closes it. STUART reads. BRAD flings himself down on his seat. Sits. Lies. Tries different positions. STUART reads.

BRAD: What does it say?

STUART: Read it and you'll find out.

BRAD: No I want you to tell me Stoosy-Woosy. Tell me what the book says about the death of Christopher Marlowe.

STUART: I don't know Brad. It says all sorts of things.

BRAD: Like what?

A beat.

Like what?

A beat.

Like what? Like what? Like what? Like what? Like what? Like what? Like what? Like what? Like what? Like what?...

STUART sighs and gives up trying to read.

STUART: Ok. Ok. Ok!!!

He stretches.

Well – it's fantastically interesting about the period. It's – it's full of detail – especially about the secret service – and –

BRAD: They had a secret service?

STUART: Yeah. They ran spies all over Europe. It was very sophisticated. Anyway it seems that Marlowe was –

BRAD: A spy right?

STUART: Yeah. At least that's the theory.

BRAD: You know what I think? I read this book once about how Shakespeare maybe wasn't Shakespeare.

STUART: Aha. Who did they say he was?

BRAD: It didn't say that. It just put the evidence for the possibilities of him being someone else. Know what I mean?

STUART: Sure. There's been lots and lots of –

BRAD: And one of the people –

STUART: Was Marlowe.

BRAD: No – they didn't think he was Marlowe but I thought he could have been Marlowe. I remember thinking that. You know? Maybe he was Marlowe.

STUART absorbs this.

STUART: Yeah well there's a whole school of thought about that. Some people think he was Marlowe, some people think he was the Earl of Oxford, some people think he was Bacon –

BRAD: And some people think he was Liberace. What difference does it make?

STUART smiles and returns to his book.

I bet you did some of his plays. Right?

STUART: Marlowe's? Yeah. I've done two.

BRAD: Two?! Wow! Which ones?

STUART: *Tamburlaine* and *The Jew Of Malta*.

BRAD gets up and spreads his arms wide, filling as much of the trailer as he can. He begins to declaim.

BRAD: 'Black is the beauty of the brightest day;
The golden ball of heavens eternal fire,
That danced with glory on the silver waves,

Now wants the fuel that inflamed his beams,
And all with faintness and for foul disgrace –

The walkie-talkie crackles into ear-splitting splutter.

BRAD: See? Micky should have lent me that book.

STUART: How come you know that?

BRAD reaches for the walkie-talkie still talking in his high flown Marlovian voice.

BRAD: I know everything Stuart! Yes! Everything you little fuck! I know every line of every play that was ever written!

He clicks the switch on the walkie-talkie.

Yeah Chris.

Indecipherable, ear-splitting splutter.

BRAD: No he's not. Pepe says Romero's unwell and in the toilet.

Indecipherable, ear-splitting splutter.

BRAD: No. Like I said I'll go to make up when it looks like we're going to do something.

Indecipherable, ear-splitting splutter.

BRAD: Chris – let me tell you something. The weather's never going to clear! It's going to rain forever and we're going to be here forever – lost and alone and desperate! You're going to be up there in the cold and the wet and we're going to be down here staring into space and quoting plays at each other. Forever Chris! Don't you understand? You poor dumb fuck? It's over! Can't you see? Tamburlaine's dead! Zenocrate's dead! Everyone's dead! They're dead! Now all of Asia must pay their just demands!

BRAD hangs up.

STUART: Where did you train?

BRAD: Lots of places.

STUART: Like where?

BRAD: See, if you look at the verse structure of some of
Marlowe's plays it's very similar to early Shakespeare.
Know what I mean? Like *Titus Andronicus* or *Henry VI*? It's
got the same bounce – sort of –

A beat.

STUART: Bouncy?

BRAD: Right.

STUART puts the book down. He thinks for a moment.

STUART: But it's really very different.

BRAD: Oh?

STUART: Yeah. I mean the Marlowe you were just quoting is
very different from the sort of thing Shakepeare wrote.

BRAD: In what way?

STUART: Ok. Well – for a start there's no real psychology in
the writing.

BRAD: Sure there is. There's lots of psychology.

STUART: No there's not. It's wonderful poetry but it's all
rhetorical verse.

BRAD: Ok – do some stuff from *Titus Andronicus*.

STUART: I can't – I don't know any but –

BRAD: 'Speak, my Lavinia, what accursèd hand
Hath made thee handless in thy fathers sight?
What fool hath added water to the sea,
Or brought a–'

STUART shakes his head in disbelief.

STUART: Ok – brilliant. I don't know how you know all this but –

BRAD: So what's the difference with that and the other stuff?

STUART: Well for a start the other stuff has six beats to the line and the Shakespeare's only got five.

BRAD: That's garbage Stuart. Listen:

He beats out the rhythm of the lines as he says them.

'Holl-a you pam-pered jades of A-si-a
What can you draw but twenty miles a day?'

Ok? Now the Shakespeare:

'Speak, my Lavinia, what accursèd hand
Hath made thee handless in thy fathers sight?'

Five and five right? There's no difference.

A beat.

STUART: Actually you're right – they do both have five.

BRAD: And even if they didn't – who cares? So, which has psychology and which doesn't?

STUART: Well I can't comment on two fragments like that. I'm talking generally.

BRAD: But based on what Stuart? Who told you one had psychology and the other didn't? Some English fag director?

STUART: Well I suppose yes – but the thing is –

BRAD: The thing is you don't really know Stuart. Someone told you something that wasn't true and you believed them – right? Some useless, talentless jerk, who wouldn't know a piece of psychology if it sat on his face, told you that Marlowe was all rhetoric and Shakespeare was all character and you believed him. Who gives a fuck if it's got six beats or five? Know what I mean?

STUART: Ok – ok you win. I can't contradict you because I don't remember any of the lines but I still say you're wrong.

He returns to the book.

BRAD: So you acted the Marlowe without psychology? Did you act it rhetorically?

STUART: No of course not –

BRAD: Because I don't know what that is.

STUART: Listen I just told you we _

BRAD: Do some for me.

STUART: What do you mean?

BRAD: Do some rhetorical acting for me. Go ahead – act rhetorically.

STUART: Piss off!

BRAD: You just said the plays were written without psychology. You said the verse was rhetorical – so do some rhetorical acting. I mean it. I'm really interested.

STUART: Brad there's no such thing. When we did those plays –

BRAD: Where did you do them?

STUART: One was in London and the other was –

BRAD: Ok – and they told you to act them rhetorically did they?

STUART: This is the most stupid conversation I've ever had! Of course not. When we did those plays we tried to make them as real as anything else – obviously! We're not idiots! All I'm saying is there's a difference in the style of writing. Can't you see that? – Maybe I'm using the wrong words – but I'd say the Shakespeare seems more complex in its psychology. That's all. It's got nothing to do with the way you act it.

BRAD: So what difference does it makes how many beats are in the line?

STUART: Not a lot. You just need a bit more breath for six instead of five.

BRAD: A bit more breath?

STUART: Yes.

BRAD: I see. Ok – so what I'm saying right now is quite a long sentence and may go this way and that and have all kinds of changes of thought in it but – I just say it? See what I'm saying? I just say it. I don't think about when I'm going to breath. So why do it on stage?

STUART: Because it's verse and you have – you have to obey certain rules when you speak it – otherwise it gets all broken up.

BRAD: What's wrong with all broken up? Brando broke it up in *Julius Caeser*.

STUART: That's not true – he went right to the end of the line. But what's the point of having verse if it's spoken like prose?

BRAD: What's the point of having verse if you can't understand what the fuck is happening and everyone's acting rhetorically?

STUART: None. If that's the case then – you're right – there's no point at all.

BRAD: I'm just questioning the rules Stuart – that's all. I don't accept that you can't breath when you want and I don't accept all this shit about metre and beats and five and six and blah blah blah – know what I mean?

STUART: Ok – fine! Breath when you want and speak it like it was written in the Bronx! I don't give a shit!

STUART goes back to his book. Half to himself BRAD starts to speak some verse in a heavy Italian Bronx accent.

BRAD: 'This royal throne of kings, this sceptered isle,
This earth of majesty, this seat of Mars,
This other Eden, demi-paradise;
This –'

STUART looks up.

STUART: Proves my point I think.

BRAD: Why? What's wrong with that?

STUART: Oh shit!

BRAD: No come on Stuart – what's wrong with that?

STUART: There's nothing wrong with it!

BRAD: Well there obviously is or you wouldn't have used that snotty tone of voice. What point does it prove?

STUART: It proves it's possible to say the stuff any way you want. Ok?

BRAD: But you don't want to hear it like that?

STUART: It's not a question of –

BRAD: You want it spoken like some prancing prince. Like some fairy who just walked out of an elocution class?

STUART: Oh Christ! Here we go.

BRAD: What?

STUART: I mean – why're you all so threatened?!

BRAD: Us all? Who's –?

STUART: It's your first line of attack. Something's a bit different so it's got to be faggy –

BRAD: Wait a minute Stuart. Don't start trying to –

STUART: – or wimpy or pussy or girly! Why?

BRAD: That's not what I meant Stuart and don't make this a redneck thing because that won't wash. You're talking to me now. Ok?

STUART: Yeah but you're not just attacking me. You're attacking something that you see as quintessentially English.

BRAD: Quinty what? I'm not attacking anything! Ok? I'm just questioning a few of your rules. Why's that so –

STUART: Everything's based on some desperate quest for masculinity. Everything's got to be –

BRAD: What is this?

STUART: – presented as streetwise and cool and –

BRAD: Listen Stuart we're getting off the point here –

STUART: No. That's the point. We're not.

BRAD: Ok. What is the point?

STUART: The point is that –

BRAD: What?

STUART: The point is that these plays were written in another century. Ok?

BRAD stares at him in mock astonishment.

BRAD: Oh. Really?!!! I never knew that.

STUART: They're not about the Bronx and they're not about the South or Chicago or anywhere else. They're not about now.

BRAD: So what's the point of doing them?

A beat.

STUART: Listen–

BRAD: If they're not about now and – ?

STUART: Sorry – I didn't mean that. Of course they relate to now – one hundred per cent – but they're not colloquial.

BRAD: I never said they were.

STUART: And we have to find some way of doing them that makes sense.

BRAD: Obviously.

A beat.

STUART: So, in that case, why would I want them spoken like a prancing prince?

BRAD: Because – because – I'll tell you why Stuart. Because – what you can't take is us wanting to do them. You –

STUART: Us?

BRAD: Americans?

STUART: Bollocks!

BRAD: No. You think we're stupid and backward and –

STUART: That's completely untrue!

BRAD: – crude and you resent it. You want us to learn all the stupid rules you did and the moment we –

STUART: You're twisting my argument.

BRAD: – question anything we're stepping out of line –

STUART: That's idiotic!

BRAD: – because Shakespeare's about the only thing your country has left!

A beat.

STUART: Sorry?

BRAD: Yeah. You got a whole lot of history and a whole lot of books. You have the past.

A beat while STUART absorbs this.

STUART: Why're you evading the issue? –

BRAD: What issue?

STUART: That verse is verse. It's not prose and it's not improvised. It's verse. It has rhythm and meter and structure. It's not casual or streetwise. It's verse and should be treated as verse.

BRAD: You got it!

STUART: And you don't want to do that because, by your own admission, you equate it with something faggy and effeminate.

BRAD: No! That's not it Stuart! Why're you putting words in my mouth? I was questioning how it's spoken not the –

STUART: But that's what we're talking about isn't it!? We're talking about the way it's spoken! I mean what else is there? Anyone can read it!

BRAD: Listen – asshole – you were the one who just said speak it like it was written in the Bronx! I did that – as a joke – you know? – and I think it sounded pretty good!

A knock at the door.

STUART: Only because you felt comfortable –

BRAD: What's wrong with that?

STUART: Nothing. Listen. All I'm saying is you can't act it colloquially because it isn't written colloquially! I said nothing about princes or fairies or elocution classes! Ok?!!!

STUART opens the door. PEPE stands outside with a plastic mac over his head. He is holding two boxes. He passes them to STUART.

Thanks Pepe. Lunch.

BRAD: Tell him to get me a beer will you? Hey – Pepe, can I have a beer? What's a beer in Spanish Stuart?

PEPE: Le voy a Llenar las botas con puntas de fierro y meter le una rata en los pantalones!

BRAD: What did he say?

STUART: Roughly translated, he said 'I'm going to fill his boots with spikes and put a rat in his pants!'

The door slams shut. BRAD goes to the door, opens it and shouts into the rain.

BRAD: Pepe! Pepe!

STUART puts BRAD's lunch box on the table and moves up to his end. He opens his box and examines the contents. He takes out some pizza. BRAD slams the door and settles into his seat. He starts to examine the contents of his lunch box.

BRAD: So how come you can't remember a single fucking line of Shakespeare Stuart?

STUART is lost.

STUART: What?

BRAD: You're the one who thinks we should all be watching the stuff and you're the one who's been prancing around the stages of Europe in a pair of tights. You want to play Othello and Lear and all the others – so how come you can't remember a single line?

STUART: I could quote you hundreds of lines –

BRAD: Ok – go ahead. (*A beat.*) I'm waiting.

STUART eats and ponders.

STUART: Ok – um – Richard II.

BRAD: Aha. Can you throw me the salt?

STUART throws him a salt cellar from the shelf and starts.

STUART: 'We are amazed; and thus long have we stood
To watch the fearful bending of thy knee, –'

BRAD: Great! I love this speech.

BRAD opens his lunch box and takes out a plastic cup of soup. He takes off the lid, has a taste and makes a face.

STUART: '– Because we thought ourselves thy lawful king:'

BRAD: What's this?

STUART: Gaspacho.

BRAD: Gas-what?

STUART: 'And if we be how dare thy joints forget
To pay their awful duty to our presence?'

BRAD: It's like a dog threw up in my cup.

STUART: 'If we be not,' – um – um – shit – 'if we be not, –'

BRAD prompts him while tasting the Gaspacho again.

BRAD: '– if we be not, show us the hand of God
That has dismissed us from our stewardship;
For well we know no hand of blood and bone –'

STUART: 'Can gripe the sacred handle of our sceptre,
Unless he do profane, steal, or usurp'.

BRAD is still preoccupied with the Gaspacho.

BRAD: It's like some lizard regurgitated yesterday's prey –

STUART: 'And though you think that all, as you have done,'

BRAD: – put it in the ice box and served it for lunch.

STUART: 'Have torn their souls by turning them from us,
And we are barren and bereft of friends;'

BRAD: This is frozen barf!

STUART: 'Yet know, my Master, God omnipotent,
Is mustering in His clouds, on our behalf,'

BRAD moves up the trailer and rummages in STUART's box.

BRAD: Did you get any potato chips?

BOTH: 'Armies of pestilence; and they shall strike
    Your Children yet unborn and unbegot,'

BRAD finds a packet of crisps. He brandishes them.

BRAD: Fucking favouritism!

He rips the packet open and crams a handful into his mouth.

STUART: 'That lift your vassal hands against my head,
    And threat the glory of my precious crown'.

STUART has arrived at the good bit and BRAD can't hold back. Pointing vigorously down the trailer, he joins in, his mouth full of pizza and crisps.

BOTH: 'Tell Bolinbroke – for yond methinks he stands,
    That every stride he takes upon my land
    Is dangerous treason: he is come to ope
    The purple testament of bleeding war;
    But, ere the crown he looks for live in peace,
    Ten thousand bloody crowns of mother's sons
    Shall ill become the flower of England's face,
    Turn her complexion of maid pale peace
    To scarlet indignation; and bedew her pastures green
    With faithful English blood'.

BLACKOUT

SCENE THREE

Later.

The rain is heavier than ever. In the blackout the walkie-talkie suddenly blurts angrily into life. A long stream of indecipherable babble follows. Then:

> *Lights up quickly. BRAD is standing in the middle of the trailer holding the walkie-talkie in one hand and his open script in the other. The babble stops. BRAD speaks into it.*

BRAD: But, listen Derek, I don't follow your line of thinking. Scene 117's an interior! It's supposed to be in Moctezuma's palace! It's our big fight! With the gold and all! How's it going to work in the open?

> *A stream of babble follows and then a click. Derek has gone. BRAD hurls the walkie-talkie across the trailer.*

BRAD: Fuck it!! Fuck this fucking film and fuck everybody in it! Fuck the fucking weather and fuck the stupid fucking English director!

> *BRAD hurls himself into his seat. A beat.*

STUART: I suppose Derek's really up against it.

> *Pause.*

> I mean he's got to do something. If he can't do your scene and he can't do the fort I suppose —

BRAD: So you think this is a good idea right?

STUART: No I think it's a terrible idea. It's just that —

BRAD: You can see Derek's predicament.

STUART: Actually — I can.

BRAD: Well that's good Stuart. I'm really glad that you feel that way.

> *A beat.*

BRAD: See, the difference between you and me is, I can see his predicament too but it doesn't interest me.

STUART: Fine.

BRAD: No it's not fine. It's not fine Stuart! It's not fucking fine!!!! His predicament is that he's panicking because he's got to get some stuff in the can or the studio will be on his back. I can see that! I'm not an imbecile. It's a tough one and I'm sorry for him. However – and this is the point so listen up – the point is that Derek doesn't see our predicament. That's the point. He doesn't see our fucking predicament and he never will.

BRAD pulls a scotch bottle from his bag. He pours some into a plastic cup but doesn't offer any to STUART.

STUART: How do you know?

BRAD: Because he's an asshole! He has absolutely no idea how actors work! You heard what he just said. I tried to discuss it and he cut me off. He didn't want to know. You heard that.

STUART: Yeah but –

BRAD: Not yeah but anything Stuart. You think he'd have talked to De Niro that way.? 'It's very wet up here Bobby and we can't do the other scenes so I'd like you to have a look at scene 117. Yes I know it's an interior but I think it'll work fine in the rain'

He imitates de Niro's voice.

'Oh that's very interesting Derek. I can see your predicament and I think the best plan is to do exactly what you say because I have no creative opinion about the film we're making and I'm happy to do everything your way. Give me a moment to learn my lines and change my shirt and I'll see you soon. Glad to be of service'.

STUART laughs.

Yeah it's funny except it's not.

STUART reaches for the bottle. BRAD grabs it and wags a 'naughty-naughty' finger. STUART shrugs.

It's so stupid! I've made more than twenty films and I've been in lots of plays, and a million TV shows. I've been to class all my life, and I've given more thought to the hows and whys of our business than a whole lot of people. But when it comes to having a voice in the process I get 'don't you worry about my line of thinking Brad. You just learn the scene because we're running late and I haven't time to discuss it'.

Pause.

And what's going to be the result? The result is going to be that one of the best scenes in this film is going to be scuttled before it starts. No matter how much we try it'll look like something out of a cheap TV show. And why? Because it's FUCKING RAINING!!! Doesn't that sicken you?

STUART: Yes. But I suppose I've grown pretty used to not being a star and pretty used to taking the shit that goes with it.

BRAD: Yeah well maybe that's the difference between us.

Pause.

Your attitude is so fucking – English. You know?

STUART: And your attitude is so fucking – American.

Pause. STUART gets his script out of his bag.

See, my experience of stars is that they have one interest and one interest only – and that's them.

STUART opens the script at the right page. BRAD stares out at the rain.

LA's like Ancient Rome. They're different versions of the same dream. Like Rome, the Hollywood dream expects you to use all your skills, all your attributes, all your experience, all your resources and cunning, to scrabble to the top of a foetid, phoney society so you can parade yourself, in some futile way, through the streets of the city in order to maintain one thing. Your status. And that's what every actor in Hollywood is doing. You're all obsessed – not with theatre or movies or art – but with your own status.

BRAD: And you're not?

STUART: I don't think it matters to me in quite the ball-aching way it does to you – no.

BRAD: Right.

Pause. BRAD takes a gulp of scotch.

BRAD: You know what's a real pain?

STUART: What?

BRAD: This trailer.

Slightly mystified STUART looks around the trailer. He nods not quite sure why he's nodding.

STUART: Jesus! There's a leak in that corner now. I never noticed that.

BRAD: There's a leak in every corner Stuart. That's not my point. What I want to know is – how come there's two of us sitting in it?

STUART: Is this an existential question?

BRAD: You can look at it that way if you want. What does your contract say about trailers?

STUART: I can't remember.

BRAD: You can't remember if you're supposed to have your own trailer?

STUART: Well I think there's something about it but since we've always been at the base before, I've always just shared with whoever they put me in with.

BRAD: I see. And today that's me. Right?

STUART: Yeah – I suppose so – well there's only one trailer here isn't there?

BRAD: That's right. There's only one trailer here Stuart.

STUART: Apart from that stupid tent thing. What's the point you're trying to make?

BRAD sighs.

BRAD: This is my trailer Stuart. Ok?

STUART looks confused. BRAD pours himself another scotch.

Yes. I have it in my contract that I should have a motor home at my disposal at all times. I always have that. The last picture I did – the one with Stallone – I had one the same size as his. You know? With a shower and a double bed – everything. I always have that. Always. Now it so happens that there's never been a motor home on this penis of a movie because either these people can't find one or they refuse to pay for one. So they've given me this trailer which leaks and stinks. However it happens to be mine.

There is a silence. STUART looks uncomfortable.

I've given up complaining but I'm within my rights to ditch the picture if I want. I spoke to my agent a few days ago and he told me to walk but – you know – what's the point?

There is a pause and then STUART picks up his stuff and makes for the door.

BRAD: Where you going?

STUART: The tent.

STUART opens the door revealing the pouring rain. He starts to go out of it.

BRAD: Don't be a stupid fuck. Come back.

STUART: Why? It's obviously a problem for you.

BRAD: I just wanted you to know that's all.

STUART: Why?

BRAD shrugs.

Why did you want me to know?

BRAD: Look it's not a problem. Ok?

STUART: Then why did you bring it up?

BRAD: I just wanted you to know.

STUART: That you have your own trailer?

BRAD: Yeah.

STUART: I see. Well thanks for telling me. I apologise for trespassing on your property.

STUART walks out into the rain holding his script over his head.

BRAD: Oh Jesus!

BRAD goes to the door and calls after him.

Stuart! Stuart! Come back here. Don't go to the tent for Christ's sake! I like you being here!

STUART calls from outside, his voice receding as he walks away.

STUART: (*Off.*) You obviously don't or you wouldn't have brought it up.

BRAD: Listen I do – I'm sorry – I didn't mean to offend you. I was just trying to –

STUART: (*Off.*) What? Just trying to what?

BRAD: Come back and we'll talk about it.

There is a pause.

Please. Come back.

After a beat STUART climbs rapidly back into the trailer. Soaking wet and furious, he stands in the middle of the trailer dripping on to the floor. His wig is a mess.

STUART: I can't believe you just said all that Brad. Jesus! We've been making this film for five weeks and – this isn't the first time I sat in your trailer for Christ's sake! I never questioned who it belonged to because – I don't know – because –

BRAD: Because what Stuart?

STUART: Because you led me to believe it was sort of available! So I imagined – you know – I imagined that –

BRAD: You imagined what?! YOU IMAGINED WHAT?! Listen Stuart lets get this straight. You've been in this trailer because I like you. Ok? I like you. No other reason. If we weren't friends you'd be in the tent with the others. Do you notice them coming in here?

STUART: Sometimes. There were four of us in here yesterday.

BRAD: That's right. There were. But only because I invited them in. Ok?

STUART: You didn't invite them in. They –

BRAD: Ok I didn't send formal invites but if I'd wanted to be on my own I only had to say.

STUART: Say what?

BRAD: Jesus! How many fucking movies have you made?

STUART: I don't know – several.

BRAD: And you always just sit in the star's trailer do you?

STUART: No of course not. Hang on – What are you saying?

BRAD: I'm saying that –

STUART: You're saying that you're the star of this film? Right?

BRAD: No I'm not saying that. Ricky's the star of this film. But I have equal –

STUART: What? Standing? Status? Billing? What?

BRAD: Ok – fine. What billing do you have?

STUART: I can't remember exactly.

BRAD: Oh come on. Sure you can.

STUART: Ok. I've got my own card on the credits.

BRAD: Right. Jesus you fucking English piss me off! How about the paid advertising? The poster? What do you have on that?

STUART: I'm not on the poster. None of the English are.

BRAD: Ok – well I am. Get it? When this movie goes out the poster will say 'Cortes' starring Richard Manes and then my name follows his – admittedly not in the same size type – but underneath. Now it may say 'with Brad Masco' or it may say 'co-starring Brad Masco' – that still has to be negotiated – but my name will be second on the poster. And my name will be second on the credits and it goes without saying that I too have a solo card. Ok? So don't give me this shit about me not starring in this movie because to all intents and purposes I am.

STUART shakes his head and makes for the door. BRAD grabs him.

BRAD: And don't go off into the rain again you asshole! I'm trying to explain something!

STUART: I think you've explained very well. You obviously find it increasingly annoying to spend your days with someone of lower status –

BRAD: Will you cut that out! You're the one who brought that up. Status this and status that! I never mentioned the fucking word!

STUART: So why does it matter so much who's trailer this is and what billing we have?

BRAD: Because it's all we've got!!!! Can't you see that?!!! It's all we've got!!!!!!

Pause.

STUART: That's pathetic.

BRAD: Maybe it is – but everything's pathetic. The whole world's pathetic Stuart!

STUART: I mean it's pathetic if you think that billing and trailers are all we've got.

BRAD: Ok so what else is there? What else is there that lets you know you're somebody?

STUART: You mean you're not somebody without all that?

BRAD: Oh come on – don't get all Gestalt on me! Why can't you just admit that you want a bit of clout like everybody else? Christ knows you've worked for it. 'I'm playing Hamlet but that's ok. I don't want my own dressing room – I'll just change with the extras. Sure I've got a few more lines than you but – so what? Come on everybody – we're all one big family – let's change tights together Crapola!! Bullshit!!! English bullshit!!!!

STUART: You said all that – not me. It's not what I think.

BRAD: No? Then what do you think?

A beat.

STUART: See – what you can't take is anyone questioning the values of Hollywood?

BRAD: I'm not talking about Hollywood!

STUART: Yes – you are. You are! Listen – first of all – I'm
sorry about the trailer. I mean it.

BRAD: Forget the trailer –

STUART: I can't forget the trailer Brad because that's why
we're having this argument! I'm sorry I took advantage of
your hospitality –

BRAD: You didn't take advantage of anything! All I'm saying
is –

STUART: Let me finish will you – I'm sorry about that and
I'm sorry that you don't have the motor home you should
have. Really. I am.

BRAD: Well thanks. That's very –

STUART: You're obviously as much a victim of these people as
me. But there's nothing I can do about it. If I could I would
– but I've spent nine tenths of my working life in grubby
halls and flea-bitten dressing rooms making do and not
complaining – because – because that was the name of the
game. We don't make a fuss – because we know there's no
alternative on offer.

BRAD: Jesus!

STUART: Do you think the English on this film had any choice
about trailers and billing and money? No they didn't. Your
beloved Hollywood producers came to England to cast
this pile of shite because they knew they'd be getting good
actors at the cheapest prices. Ok? Otherwise why didn't
they cast it in the States?

BRAD: Well maybe they –

STUART: They knew they could offer us rock bottom
conditions at rock bottom money and no one would
complain – or if they did they could get some other poor
schmuck with the wave of a hand. The reason we don't
have any clout – as you put it – is because your country
has the whole stinking industry sewn up. You make the

films, you control the cinemas, you own the distributors and you get ninety percent of the profits.

BRAD: And tomorrow we bomb Poland.

STUART: Why not? You bombed everywhere else. Now, it so happens that once a year we do actually manage to make a film in England and it usually wins an Oscar – whatever that means – but do we get any more of the cake or even the chance to make another one?

BRAD: Is this a rhetorical question?

STUART: No. All it means is the same dreary process has to start again – going round with the hat for a thousand here and ten thousand there till maybe – just maybe – there's enough to start work again, and when that happens – when one of us luckless idiots happens to get a part in one of those films – do you think we get paid? Do me a favour! I mean compared with the money you make it's a joke! See we don't play the status game because we don't have any status to play it with. Now – whatever you say – this trailer business is to do with status. The trailers, the billing, the entourage, the PR men, the lawyers, the personal managers, the cooks, the masseuses, the chauffeurs and the psychotherapists are all part of some Roman type deal that informs others you're now a cut above them. You've arrived. Well we haven't arrived and that's why we're still in the fucking tent! It's also why eight of my countrymen are, at this moment, sitting in a clapped out minibus on the side of some dirt track in the pouring, stinking rain! Do you think they like that? Do you think they like changing in a filthy tent or accepting your magnanimity when you choose to invite them in for tea? Do you really believe they're any less talented or experienced than you are? Do you think they don't care about not having a fucking trailer? Of course they do! But what they want is to earn a living and – maybe – in the meantime do some decent work. Now you can mock our apparent acquiescence, and you can abuse our interest in the classics, but know this.

You do it from the vantage of a society that is spoiled, corrupt, greedy and ignorant – and, as a highly intelligent and sensitive person, I think you should know better!

STUART walks out into the rain. BRAD goes to the door and shouts.

BRAD: You pompous Asshole!!

STUARTs voice floats back through the rain.

STUART: (*Off.*) I'm going to the tent Brad. That's where I belong.

BRAD: Good. I hope the roof falls in on you.

STUART: (*Off.*) Fuck you!

PEPE rushes into the trailer carrying more costume.

BRAD: O Christ! Not you!

PEPE: Brad deves preperar te. Dora dice que tienes que llevar todo – tu capa, la armura – todo! Ven para ayudarte. Tienes que ir a maquillarte pero ahora mismo.

There is a beat while BRAD stares at him.

Brad? Por favor vete a maquillarte!

BRAD screams in frustration.

BRAD: I – can't – under-stand – a – sing-le- word – you're – saying!

PEPE: Bueno, no vayas a maquillarte Senor Boca Grande recto Americano de Puerco! Dora dice que yo le debo de vestir. Yo Perdere mi trabajo si llegas tarde al esenario – sube los brazos (mendigo hijo de puta) y saca la cabeza (de perro enfermo) y a ver si le puedo poner este blindaje! Asqueroso! Es que no se sabe lavar? Se llama jabon! Apesta a cono podrido!

He pushes and tugs and presses the remaining leather and armour onto BRAD, who furiously begins to cooperate. PEPE starts to place BRAD's sword.

Espero que esta espada pentetre su peritoneo! Y que este punal se empene en sus testiculos! Espero que sus miserables dedos de salchicha crezcan telaranas al tocar su-

BRAD: Not there! I hate it there! Twist it round! See? Like that! How can I get the knife out if – no! Like that! Jesus! Let me do this myself will you!

PEPE stands back while BRAD attempts to wrestle with his armour.

Your friend Romero does this soooo much better.

PEPE: Romero esta en el hospital.

BRAD understands the word.

BRAD: Hospital?

PEPE: Si! Hospital! Romero esta muy enfermo.

BRAD: So I'm stuck with you. Great.

BRAD grabs his script from the table and shouts across his shoulder at the still open door.

BRAD: Stuart!

A beat. No reply.

Stuart! What are you doing?

No reply. PEPE continues to dress BRAD.

Stoosy Woosy! This is Bradly-Wadly! We've got to do our sceeny-weeny Stoosy Woosy!

A beat. BRAD leafs through the script to scene 117.

Oh come on Stuart! Are we going to work on this or not?

STUART's voice is heard in the distance. It is slightly muffled from being inside the tent.

STUART: (*Off.*) Ok let's do it.

A beat.

You've got the first line.

BRAD: I'm not going to read it like this Stuart. Come over here.

STUART: (*Off.*) This suits me fine Brad. Why don't you come over here?

A beat.

BRAD: You stupid English scumbag! (*To PEPE.*) This is all tangled up for Chissakes!

PEPE straightens whatever it is.

STUART: (*Off.*) I never realised how pleasant this tent was. I must have been mad to go anywhere else.

A beat.

BRAD: Ok, I'm not going to stand here like a dick trying to be nice. Let's do it.

STUART: (*Off.*) Go on then.

BRAD: It's you.

STUART: (*Off.*) Aren't you going to say your first line then?

BRAD: What for? It doesn't make any sense now. 'Put that back Sandoval' – that's a line from inside the palace – you know – when I see you with the gold helmet or whatever. How can I say that if we're outside?

STUART: (*Off.*) I don't know. Let's just read it as it is. We can work out what to change afterwards.

BRAD: Shit! Shit shit shit shit! Ok.

He starts to shout the scene into the rain. STUART's voice comes back on cue.

BRAD: 'Put that back Sandoval!'

STUART: (*Off.*) 'My son put up your sword. This treasure must be sequestered in the name of our Redeemer'.

BRAD: 'In the middle of the night? With a sack'?

STUART: (*Off.*) 'This is holy work'.

BRAD: 'And this is their holiest shrine'.

STUART: (*Off.*) 'Nothing of the heathen is holy. Our work here has barely begun. Think of what we can bring these people! Pagan gold for Christian salvation!'

BRAD continues to read but holds his foot in the air. He points out the hole in his boot to PEPE.

BRAD: 'Pagan gold for your own pocket you mean! Your holy pose may deceive Cortes but it never fooled me. You're nothing but a treacherous, barbarous thief!'

BRAD shouts at PEPE.

Fucking hole!! How can I walk round with that?

STUART: (*Off.*) 'Listen Gonzalez. Listen to me. When I left Salamanca I promised my wife I'd make her rich' –

PEPE: Usted mismo hizo el agujero! – Usted! Rayo grande de mierda! Yo lo vi hacer lo!

BRAD: I asked someone to mend it! – 'Ha! A priest with a wife? So a blasphemer too!'

STUART: (*Off.*) 'Brave words from a Salamancan whore master!'

BRAD: But nobody did. Ok? Nobody did!

PEPE shrugs.

'I was once a whore master Sandoval and I paid the price. Your friends in the Inquisition saw to that! But now I'm a soldier – a soldier of the crown. In the name of King Carlos the Fifth I command you to replace that gold'.

STUART: (*Off.*) 'Your commands fall on deaf ears Diego!'

A beat.

Then I draw my sword and you draw yours and we fight and you kill me and that's that.

BRAD: Yeah. That's that.

A beat.

That's fucking that.

A beat.

This is a piece of shit!

STUART: (*Off.*) Tell me about it!

PEPE starts to leave.

BRAD: Hey – what about my boot? Pepe?

PEPE turns at the door.

PEPE: Espero que sus botas de mierda se conviertan en un foso septico!

BRAD: I want someone to mend this fucking boot!!!!!

But PEPE has gone. BRAD gives up and reverts to shouting across to STUART.

BRAD: I mean – I can hardly get these stupid words out of my mouth.

A beat.

Have you learned this?

STUART: (*Off.*) Sort of.

BRAD: Fuck!

A beat.

Ok well I think I'm going to pour myself a nice big Scotch and try and learn this garbage too Stuart. Bye now.

BRAD pours a generous slug of scotch into a paper cup, sits down and starts to look at the script. The rain hammers on the roof as the walkie-talkie splutters into life.

Indecipherable, ear-splitting splutter.

BRAD: Emilio? No – he's not here yet. We're waiting. All tooled up and ready to go.

Indecipherable, ear-splitting splutter.

BRAD: He left forty minutes ago?!! Doesn't he have a radio in his car?

Indecipherable, ear-splitting splutter. BRAD hangs up. STUART appears at the door holding his script over his head.

BRAD: Apparently Emilio should have been here twenty minutes ago.

STUART picks up the bottle. BRAD doesn't stop him. STUART helps himself to a liberal measure of scotch. BRAD talks without looking up from the script. The atmosphere is as though nothing had happened.

I mean the whole point of this scene is it's supposed to be in a room full of gold. It's the king's chamber. The inner sanctum. Right?

STUART: Right.

STUART takes a gulp of scotch and his eyes close with intense pleasure.

BRAD: I haven't seen the designs but I'd imagined a strange circular, vault with an echo – you know? A spooky kind of an echo. Just the two of us in this weird, sacred building. A vast golden space. Me at one end – you at the other.

Real distance between us. You filling a sack with stuff and me begging you to stop in the name of the church and the crown and all and, as you don't stop, I draw nearer. Right? Closer and closer across a golden floor till we're facing each other. Closer and closer through all the swinging asure, weird jungle sounds outside, the gleam of a million precious stones –

STUART: Strange magical maps on the golden walls –

BRAD: Images of their Gods everywhere –

STUART: A vast feathered statue of Quetzacoatl.

BRAD: Right – that's a must – and everywhere there are signs of recent occupation. Whoever it was has left in haste. Fled. A golden orb hangs from the central dome. It swings in time to the earth's spin. Mysterious charts are strewn on the floor –

STUART: Astrological data, historical documents, priests puzzling it out – is this the return of Quetzacoatl? Is this the revenge of the son of the sun?

BRAD: He prophesied he'd return in the year I-Ictal, the year of the 'one reed'.

STUART: This is such a year.

BRAD: Is this his return?

STUART: Is this the end of the Aztec nation?

BRAD: Is Cortes Quetzacoatl? Who are these creatures – half men, half horse, clad in steel – who came from the East?

Pause

STUART: Instead of which we're under a tree in the rain.

He imitates Derek directing.

'Ok – very good both of you but I want to get this in a two shot if I can so, – Brad, can you move in a bit closer at the beginning'.

He imitates BRAD.

'Yeah but Derek if I'm closer at the beginning then it doesn't really give us a long way to go. See I think –'

He imitates Derek.

'Yes well I'm not really very interested in what you think Brad. The lights going, everyone's getting wet and I'd like to get this in before lunch so just do what I say. Give it lots of welly and it'll be fine. Ok? Action! '

BRAD laughs but looks depressed.

BRAD: I wish that was a joke.

STUART: I mean what's really important is to show what these bastards were taking! Two men from an alien country stand in a room full of great art and they have no idea what they're looking at. One can't wait to loot it, break it up, melt it down, – whatever – and the other commands him to stop – not because he has any appreciation of its cultural worth – but because he represents the state and a religious order that is about to ruin the Aztec civilisation. That's the point of the scene and that's why – if it was done right – it could mean something. Under a tree in the rain it just becomes a scene from a bad Western.

BRAD: You got it.

STUART: And that's why the fight between us is so important – I mean the way in which it's done.

BRAD: It should be vicious right?

STUART: Yeah. Really desperate.

BRAD: That's what I figured. We should be rolling around, smashing into things –

STUART: Exactly. I could attack you with one of the artefacts – a gold statue perhaps or –

BRAD: One of their sacrificial knives! You could –

STUART: Brilliant! That's a great idea! And maybe that's how I die! You know – maybe I trip and fall on the knife myself –

BRAD: Great! So I don't actually kill you. You kill yourself – or rather the knife –

STUART: I get stabbed accidentally.

BRAD: Right.

STUART: So there's an irony in my death?

BRAD: Right. So there's an irony in your death!

STUART helps himself to another drink. BRAD stretches out his cup and STUART refills it. STUART raises his cup in a toast.

STUART: We who are about to dry salute you.

They drink.

BRAD: God this is so depressing! I feel like I'm on death row. Why does it have to be like this?

A beat.

I mean what's happened? We're in space for Christ's sake! We're on the moon, we're deciphering DNA, we're transplanting organs, we're doing quantum this and quantum that and they're – they're putting a microchip in a parrots asshole – so what the fuck has happened that someone is able to write this?

STUART: Hang on.

STUART stares blearily at the script.

I just had an idea. I think we might be able to make this scene work –

BRAD: In the open? How for Christ's sake?

STUART: Well I mean –

STUART pours himself another large scotch and takes a slug.

See – if they 're setting it outside now – then I've presumably been to the palace, stolen the stuff, made a successful escape and somehow you've found me. Right? So what am I doing with it?

BRAD: I don't know – you're getting on your horse or you're putting it in a sack or something.

STUART: Yeah – you see – yeah – that's where we've been lazy in our thinking. What if I'm burying it?

BRAD looks interested.

BRAD: Aha?

STUART: We'd have to change some lines but –

BRAD: The image could be good. Burying it.

He thinks for a moment.

That's interesting. Yeah. We see me approaching – through the rain – I hear something –

STUART: You stop – listen – follow the sound –

BRAD: And then I see you in a clearing – digging like some dog under a tree.

STUART: I've got a sack next to me so you can guess what's going on.

BRAD: I creep up on you –

STUART: But your foot snaps a branch or something –

BRAD: You look up –

STUART: See you –

BRAD: Grab the stuff and run!

STUART: Great! Now we have a chase sequence!

BRAD: No that's no good. Derek will never buy that. There'll be no time. It's all going to have to be in the same location.

STUART: Ok. So I grab the stuff and –

BRAD: You're about to run when all the stuff spills everywhere!

STUART: That's good! Gold, silver, jewels, everything.

BRAD: So we see it! Ok now I run over and I have my sword out. I'm standing over you with it pointed at your throat.

STUART: You look at all the stuff and –

BRAD: I can't believe what I see.

STUART: Right – now scene wise you have to ask me where I got it or the audience will be confused.

BRAD: Ok so I ask and –

STUART: I lie. I say I bought it cheap from some Indians. I gave them some beads in return.

BRAD: Yeah – but I'm picking through the stuff with the point of my sword and I see some piece of gold that could only have come from the palace – something with Moctezuma's face on it. Something the priests would use maybe.

STUART: So now you challenge me – like in the original – but you tell me I have to take the stuff back. I have to take it back to the palace –

BRAD: Right. You tell me to go fuck myself and I give you all that stuff about the emperor and not being thieves and everything –

STUART: And all the time you're talking I'm reaching for a ceremonial knife that's lying with the other stuff –

BRAD: Good. You pretend to agree. Sheepishly you get to your feet and then – wham! – you let me have it!

STUART: But I miss.

BRAD: No – no! The knife hits home! But it doesn't penetrate because – because – because it hits the gold medallion – the one with Montezuma's head on I picked up earlier!

STUART: That's great! Now we fight – lots of action – really vicious like we said – and at some point I fall back –

BRAD: Right onto the ceremonial knife –.

STUART: Like we said before. Ok now I'm dead. You pull the knife out, put it into the sack with the other stuff, kick me into the grave I've unwittingly dug for myself and walk nobly off to return the treasure to the king.

BRAD: In the name of Jesus Christ and the Emperor Charles V.

A beat.

STUART: How about that?

A beat.

BRAD: Not bad. That's not bad. Ok. Let's try it.

STUART: What do you mean?

BRAD backs off and starts to mime walking through undergrowth.

BRAD: Let's rehearse it. Ok. So here I come – through the trees or whatever. The camera tracks with me – holds me in big close up. My face is alert and I'm real watchful. Suddenly I stop! What's that sound?

He listens.

I'm all ears now. I start to edge forward – slowly – slowly – through the undergrowth –

STUART gets down on his hands and knees and makes vague digging movements.

STUART: Clunk – clunk – scrape – scrape –

BRAD: Then I see you in the moonlight. Nice moody reaction shot on my face –

STUART: I don't see you 'cos I'm digging.

BRAD: Slowly – slowly I creep up on you and – 'I knew you were a criminal Sandoval but I never realised you were a blasphemer too'.

STUART turns.

STUART: Hang on! That's not in the script.

BRAD: Fuck the script.

STUART: Yeah but Derek's never going to buy a whole new version. He's –

BRAD: Stuart, I'm not playing this scene as written. Ok? It's bullshit. Derek likes my rewrites. Just make it good. He always listens.

STUART: He didn't listen just now –

BRAD: Oh don't be such a wimp! Let's do it. Ready?

Reluctantly STUART turns back to his digging.

BRAD: 'You have no right to that. It belongs to our Emperor in the name of our Holy Mother Church. You Salamancan dog!'

BRAD grabs STUART, pulls him to the floor, turns him over and sits on his chest. STUART struggles like crazy. He tries to speak.

STUART: Aaaaahhh! Brad you're – Aaaahhh!

BRAD is kneeling on STUARTs arms.

BRAD: 'You're brave when you take from the heathen but not so courageous when your Christian captain sits on your chest'.

STUART: Brad please you're – aaahhh!

BRAD: 'Why should I reason with you Sandoval? I'm sick of that. This treasure's going back where it belongs and you're going to swing from the end of a rope'.

BRAD knees press into STUARTs biceps with great force.

STUART: Aaaahhh!

BRAD: Ok this is good.

STUART: Noh-oh-OW – oooooooooh!

BRAD: I think you should say something though.

STUART: Get off me!

BRAD: No come on. It's got to be something Sandoval would say.

STUART struggles violently but is no match for BRAD's strength.

Maybe you offer to share the treasure? Try that.

STUART: Aaaahhh! You're really hurting me!

BRAD: That's pathetic. He'd never say that.

STUART: Please – I can't breathe!

BRAD: Ok.

BRAD gets up suddenly and draws an imaginary sword. STUART lies on the ground groaning and holding his arms.

'You have a choice Sandoval. Yield to the justice of the crown or take your chance with me'.

STUART: Asshole!

Rubbing his arms STUART slithers back out of BRAD's reach.

BRAD: Come on Stuart – are we doing this or not?

STUART takes a deep angry breath but then grimly decides to continue.

STUART: 'Listen Gonzalez – when I left Salamanca I promised my wife I'd make her rich – I intend to honour that –

BRAD: 'Hand it over Sandoval!'

STUART: 'Why should I? I've worked like a dog! I've suffered with hunger, thirst, sickness, terror – and for what? We came here for gold didn't we? Well I've found my share and nobody's taking it off me. Not the king, not the priests, not the –'

BRAD points his imaginary sword at STUART's throat.

BRAD: 'Hand it over!'

STUART looks at the imaginary sword point.

STUART: 'Alright Gonzalez – I'll make a deal with you! Let's split it! Half each! God man you'll be rich – look what I've got in here!'

He pretends to reach into the sack and brings out an imaginary object which he holds up to BRAD.

'It's gold! Solid gold! – studded with precious –'

BRAD grabs the object and looks at it.

BRAD: 'This is a sacred medallion. It bears Moctezuma's face'.

A beat. STUART looks puzzled.

STUART: (*As himself.*) No it's not. That's the dagger. That's the ceremonial knife.

BRAD throws his hands up in exasperation.

BRAD: You can't do that Stuart! If I say it's a medallion then it's a –

STUART: Look – this isn't a bloody improvisation class! We're trying to work out a sequence that works. We decided that I fall back on the dagger!

BRAD: So when do I get the medallion? The one that saves my life?

STUART: I don't know! That's up to you!

A beat.

BRAD: Ok. Forget it!

BRAD moves to his end and takes a drink.

Let's just forget it.

STUART: That's great! Thanks a lot Brad.

BRAD: What's the point? You just want to replace one load of cliché with another load of cliché. All that shit about your wife in Salamanca! Who cares about her?

STUART: I do. Sandoval does.

BRAD: So that's why he came to Mexico is it? To make his wife rich?

STUART: That's what it says in the script

BRAD: Fuck the script! We already decided it's garbage!

STUART: Ok so why do you care so much about the emperor and the church?

BRAD: Because we know from history that Gonzalez was the emperor's man Stuart! There're statues to him all over Mexico! Where's the statue to Sandoval's wife?

STUART: This is pointless!

BRAD: Oh sure! I say something bright and suddenly it's pointless!

STUART: Look, our version's got to be watertight. If we get up there and start bickering Derek will just tell us to go back to the original.

BRAD: Who's bickering?

STUART pours some more scotch and stares out at the rain.

A silence.

I didn't stop the scene.

STUART: No I did –

BRAD: Thank you.

STUART: – because you'd mistaken the dagger for the medallion. What's the big deal? But –

BRAD: No that's not it Stuart!

STUART: – not content with that, you then started to question my dialogue and my motivation.

BRAD: You questioned mine!

STUART: Oh give me a break! I objected to your violence. You hurt me.

BRAD: Good. Listen I didn't mistake the medallion. That's what pissed me off. It would have been a great moment for me to have –

STUART: I mean what the fuck is it with you? Why's it good that you hurt me? What's good about that?

BRAD: Oh come on! It was a joke for Christ's sake!

STUART: No it wasn't. Why did you want to hurt me? Come on! I really want to know.

STUART gets up and refills his glass. BRAD watches him.

BRAD: I think maybe we should take some time out. Ok?

STUART: I don't want some time out. I want to know why you decided to beat me up.

BRAD: I played the situation Stuart! Sorry if it got rough but that's how things were in Mexico!

STUART: Oh yeah. I forgot. Acting isn't pretending is it? It's got to be for real. So hitting's hitting, and kicking's kicking and strangling's strangling and – anyway you didn't play the situation! That's my point! If you'd done that –

BRAD: Sure I did –

STUART: Oh do me a favour! All you did was grab me round the neck while you shouted a lot of –

BRAD: Stuart let me tell you something –

STUART: – useless, unspecific, cod-historic, bullshite!'

BRAD: – you're really beginning to get on my nerves.

STUART: Wack-o.

BRAD: No I'm serious. You're getting me down now. You're making me angry.

STUART takes a big gulp of scotch and flops on his seat. BRAD picks up the walkie-talkie and clicks it.

BRAD: Chris? Chris it's Brad. Are you receiving me? Chris?

There is no answer.

STUART: Maybe you don't know your own strength.

BRAD: I think –

STUART: You know – like Lenny in –

BRAD: I do Stuart.

STUART: Of Mice And Men-

BRAD: Chris?

STUART: – crushing peoples hands and necks –

BRAD: It's Brad.

STUART: – when all he wanted was to be friends.

BRAD: What the fuck's happening? Chris?

STUART: He's gone away Brad. We're all on our own now.

BRAD puts the walkie-talkie down rather carefully.

BRAD: I know my own strength just fine.

He gets up, opens the trailer door and stares out.

At least I've got some.

STUARTs face puckers in mock distress.

STUART: Now that was uncalled for.

STUART reaches for the bottle.

Are you inferring that –?

BRAD turns, with lightning speed, and snatches the bottle out of his hand.

STUART: Hey! Give that –

BRAD: You had enough.

STUART: Says who?

BRAD stares out into the rain. STUART looks at him blearily.

What's going on?

A beat.

I was drinking from that.

STUART stands and moves a bit unsteadily towards BRAD.

BRAD: Sit down Stuart.

STUART: Why?

BRAD: You're drunk.

STUART: No I'm not.

BRAD: Sit down.

STUART: No. Who the fuck do you think you are? John Wayne?

Does a passable John Wayne impression.

'I want every man aboard this ship to have an extra ration of comic books and chewing gum and that's an order'. Jesus! You're all the same.

BRAD shoves STUART gently in the chest and he lands in his seat with a plop.

BRAD: When did you last take a drink?

STUART: Oh here we go!

BRAD: Well?

STUART: Oh I get it! Shit! How insensitive of me! The whisky's yours isn't it! Like the trailer. I've been taking another mans drink. Sorry. Hang on – I've got some cash in my –

STUART gets up but BRAD shoves him back into his seat again.

Why do you keep doing that?

BRAD: Stay there.

STUART holds up his hands in mock submission.

STUART: Whatever you say Gonzalez.

BRAD: I thought you were on the wagon.

STUART: I am.

BRAD: So why're you drinking?

STUART: Probably for the same reason you keep pushing me in the chest.

BRAD: You had enough.

STUART reaches for a paper cup.

STUART: Listen. Give us a slug and I'll take it back to the tent. Eh? That's fair. Just a drop and I'll fuck off.

BRAD: I'd like that.

STUART: Great! Come on then.

Reluctantly BRAD pours some scotch into STUART's cup.

Don't be stingy. Bit more. Up to the pretty. Lovely.

STUART takes a gulp.

Mmmmm!

BRAD opens the trailer door. STUART gets up and looks out.

Doesn't look very nice out there.

BRAD: Stuart, please – just go.

STUART: In a minute. There's something I wanted to say first though. When –

BRAD: No. You've got your drink now please –

STUART: Now don't start telling me what to do Brad because I'll –

Grabbing STUART violently by the back of his jerkin and the seat of his pants, BRAD hurls him out of the trailer and slams the door. STUART's furious voice can be heard outside.

STUART: (*Off.*) You bastard! I've spilled it now!

BRAD picks up the walkie-talkie.

BRAD: Chris? Can you come in please. Chris?

The door opens and STUART starts back into the trailer. He is covered in mud. BRAD drops the walkie-talkie and moves to him fast.

BRAD: I said I want you out!

STUART dodges him and moves rapidly back into the trailer. He furiously grabs the whisky bottle and pours himself another drink. Gulps it down. BRAD moves towards him. STUART is swaying.

STUART: So what're you going to do? Kill me? Come on then! It's late in the day, shadows are falling, we've all missed tea. Why not? Go on – give Chris a ring. Tell him to bring a camera. We'll make a little snuff film. Mind if I call my agent? Just following form. I'm sure he'll waive commission but we ought to give him the option.

BRAD lunges at him but STUART steps niftily out of his way.

No you don't! I'm not Sandoval. Ok? I'm not some Jesuit you can chuck in a hole. I'm me! I have rights! Nobody throws me in the mud! Ok? Nobody!

He takes a swig of scotch.

Of course I appreciate the urge. The pressing need to impose on those who may think otherwise. The will of the mighty. Marvellous! Fuck 'em, nuke 'em, glass 'em over! The only way! Starve 'em out! Let's kick ass!

Does John Wayne voice – even tries the walk.

'Well of all the –! Take that you Commie mutt'.

BRAD clicks the walkie-talkie again.

BRAD: Chris? Chris – for Christ's sake!

STUART: Yes come and help us Chris! Save us from ourselves!

BRAD grabs STUART's arm and starts to drag him to the door.

BRAD: You're going out and you're staying out!

STUART slips from his grasp.

STUART: Ah! The mailed fist – the steel boot. I mean you're tolerant to a point – tow that barge, lift that bale – but step over the line – it's a bridge too far. Out the door, no questions asked! We take no prisoners! The American way!

BRAD: Oh Jesus!

STUART: Of course! Jolly Jack Jesus! Absolutely! Right behind you. All the way. One of the chaps! Loves your country

– can't get enough of it! Proud of you, proud of what you
do! Yes indeedy! Damned proud! Cheers you on, cheers
you up, gets you going in the morning! No time for wimpy,
pussy people! Girls who hate guns, men with bad teeth.
No sir! The right to bear arms! The right to break legs!
The right to bomb poor people! Yes siree! That's what He
wants. That's what He died for. You're His kind of land!

BRAD: I think –

STUART: I mean – no wonder half the world hates your guts!
No wonder they can't wait to – poison your wells and –

BRAD: Stuart –

STUART: Blow up your cities and –

BRAD: I'm warning you –

STUART: Yeah?

BRAD: Don't go there! Don't go there! Don't go there!

STUART suddenly shouts.

STUART: My gran died in the Blitz you know!!

BRAD: What?

STUART: Doodlebug hit the roof. Killed half the street.

BRAD: What's that got to do with me?

STUART: How about the Granada cinema. Saturday
morning. Eight hundred kids. They collected the bodies
in cardboard boxes. Daily event mate. No speeches. No
heroes. No minutes silence.

BRAD: What are you saying?

STUART: Talk about Ground bloody Zero! Whole of England
was a bloody bomb site! In five months! Stretchers, hoses,
black outs. Fifty thousand dead. A hundred thousand
wounded – crippled, blinded. Two million homes blown

to fuck. Lives ruined. Endless grey. All that grief. All that
bottled grief. Think about it.

BRAD: I don't need to. We don't bottle our grief Stuart. We
feel it and we show it. Ok? You think about that!

STUART stares at him stupidly.

We didn't get bombed in the Blitz. Sorry. It could be
geography. Look at the map! Does that mean we lose the
right to feel? Like it's our fault you're fucked and we're not!
Is that what you're saying?

STUART: No. I'm saying that – that –

STUART sways.

BRAD: What? Come on Stuart! You seem a bit confused?

STUART: I'm not confused.

BRAD: Could have fooled me.

STUART: I'm not confused! I'll tell you what I'm – what I'm –!

BRAD: Please do.

STUART: I'm saying –

STUART grasps the wardrobe, steadies himself.

I'm saying – ok I'm saying – you can – you can dish it out
but you can't take it.

BRAD: Oh really? Take what?

STUART: This!

*STUART suddenly lunges at BRAD and kicks him hard in the crutch.
BRAD doubles up for a moment. Then, with a lightning recoil, he
whips up and hits STUART hard in the face. STUART's head clunks
against the wardrobe door and he collapses like a sack of potatoes.
He lies very still.*

BRAD: Now get up and get out!

STUART lies motionless. His head is at an odd angle.

Come on Stuart! Get up! I've had enough!

BRAD gives STUART a kick but he doesn't move.

STUART! Come on now! Don't fool around. I want you out of this trailer. Stuart?

BRAD bends over STUART's prone body.

Stuart!

BRAD starts to slap STUART round the face.

Stuart! Come on! Can you hear me?

Shakes him. There is no response. STUART's body is limp.

Oh Jesus!

BRAD picks up the walkie-talkie.

Chris! Please come in! This is Brad! Chris?

No response. BRAD stands over STUART's body. For a moment he seems paralysed. Then he makes for the door and rushes out. His voice can be heard shouting outside.

Chris? Chris? Pepe? Is anyone there? Hullo? Oh Christ! Chris!!

STUART gets slowly to his feet and staggers into the toilet. After a moment BRAD returns. He is soaking wet. He stares in bewilderment at the empty floor. Suddenly the toilet door opens. STUART jumps out and grabs BRAD round the neck.

STUART: Surprise! Made you look!

With amazing speed BRAD forces STUART's arm away, twists it behind his back and forces him up against the door of the toilet.

STUART: Aaaaahhh!

BRAD: You stupid, fucking idiot!

STUART: You're breaking my arm!

BRAD: I thought I'd killed you!

BRAD smashes STUART's body furiously against the door as he speaks.

BRAD: You shouldn't have done that! You shouldn't have done that! Why did you do that? Why'd you do it? Why did you do that?

BRAD lets go of STUART who crumples onto the floor. BRAD sits heavily on the seat.

I thought I'd killed you.

He stifles sobs.

You shouldn't have done that Stuart.

From the floor STUART stares at him in amazement.

STUART: Brad I –

BRAD: You know what it's like to kill someone? Do you? You stupid –

His sobbing increases. He seems out of control.

Oh Christ!

He rolls over, knees to chest, holding his head. STUART gets up painfully.

Oh Christ! Don't come over here Stuart.

STUART stops. BRAD rocks in misery. STUART pours a drink into a cup. He hands it to BRAD. BRAD knocks it out of his hand.

BRAD: I don't want a drink!

BRAD gets up suddenly.

That's your answer to everything isn't it?

STUART: Listen – Brad – I'm –

BRAD: Sorry? Thanks a lot! I thought I'd killed you.

BRAD opens the trailer door and breathes deeply.

STUART: I'm –

BRAD: You're an idiot. Ok? I came this close! And if I had – Jesus!

A beat.

I can't afford to get angry.

STUART: You had every right to –

BRAD: I can't afford it! I don't have any rights in that department. I did seven years. Jesus! I never learn.

STUART: Seven years?

A beat.

What for?

BRAD stares out into the rain.

You mean – you mean –?

BRAD: Yeah. That's right Stuart. I killed someone.

STUART sits down shakily. BRAD turns.

Never know who you're dealing with do you?

STUART shakes his head stupidly.

STUART: Seven years? Who was it? Sorry that's not– I mean–

BRAD: I don't want to talk about it.

STUART: Fine.

A beat.

Look maybe I should –

STUART starts to edge towards the door. BRAD is blocking his way.

BRAD: Where you going?

STUART: I'm – I thought I'd – you know –

BRAD: Make a little move?

STUART: Sort of yes.

BRAD shakes his head.

BRAD: Uh-uh.

STUART: Ok.

STUART moves back to the seat.

BRAD: I'm going to have to decide what to do with you Stuart. Yes sirree. I'm going to have to put my thinking cap on.

STUART: In what way Brad?

BRAD: In what way? Well – I never told anyone before. See what I'm saying? I never told anybody about being in jail. It's not something I'd like folks to know.

STUART: Quite right. I mean – I wouldn't want anybody to – you know – it's not –

BRAD: What are you trying to say Stuart?

STUART: I won't tell anybody Brad. I swear to Christ!

BRAD: Yeah – well – see – that's my problem. I don't know I can trust you. What with the drink and all. I mean you're not exactly –

STUART: Brad! Look at me! I'm sober! Ok? A few minutes ago I was drunk. Now I'm sober. See?

BRAD: Only 'cos you're scared. You've pissed your pants.

BRAD shakes his head.

No, I could never be sure about you Stuart. You don't know when to stop. I know your type. You got a death wish.

STUART makes a dash for the door. BRAD reaches out an arm and drags him back.

BRAD: I said no Stuart.

STUART: Brad – listen – this is ridiculous. I know I behaved abominably but –

BRAD: You behaved like a pig Stuart.

STUART: I know Brad. I –

BRAD: You insulted me, my family, my acting and my country. You insulted my country Stuart! You've been doing it all day and I'm sick of it. You think I'm a big laugh don't you?

STUART: Brad I don't! I think you're –

BRAD: What?

STUART: I think you're one of the brightest people I ever met. I do!

BRAD: Sure.

STUART: It's the truth for Christ's sake! Look what you know. All that – that Shakespeare, all that Marlowe, all that – much more than I do.

BRAD: Yeah. You know where I learned that?

STUART: Um – in jail?

BRAD: Right. I learned it in jail. I spent hours and hours – I spent years learning that stuff –

STUART: That's what I'm saying Brad. You –

BRAD: Let me finish will you! Just for once let me finish!

BRAD: When I went in there I knew nothing from nothing. Ok? I didn't come from a place where it mattered. My family weren't bright. Not their fault but they were all fucked up. Too many stupid people living in one place. I grew up on the street and it wasn't an arty neighbourhood.

I guess I was some sort of moron. My uncle was bothering my sister. He lived down the hall. I asked him to stop but he wouldn't. He'd been drinking and we got into a fight. I hit him and he went over the stair rail. Broke his neck.

A beat.

That's not what I was telling you. In jail I met this teacher. He came in twice a week and gave classes and – well I discovered I had a talent. He directed a play and gave me a part. I was the best thing in it. From there things snowballed. There were other plays and I read everything. I read Dickens and Shakespeare and Marlowe and Tolstoy and Stanislavski. Ok? I read everybody and, when I came out, I was equipped. I was totally ready. One hundred percent. I worked and I worked and I have a reputation. Ok? People think I'm smart now. Maybe because I am. I am pretty smart. I go to classes and I work hard. All the time. I read a lot and I have definite opinions.

STUART is watching him intently.

See?

A silence.

STUART: When's your wife coming?

BRAD: Maybe next week.

A beat.

How about your girlfriend? What's her name?

STUART: Cath.

BRAD: You said she was coming too.

STUART: She was.

BRAD: Aha.

A beat.

Because if they're here together they can maybe go out
– you know – or –

A beat.

STUART: Yeah.

STUART gets up and moves gingerly to the cupboard. He takes out his bag and anorak.

BRAD: What you doing?

STUART throws the Marlowe book to BRAD.

STUART: I've finished with this so you may as well have it.

BRAD looks at the book sleeve.

BRAD: 'How did Marlowe die?'

STUART: He was killed in a pub in Deptford.

BRAD: I know.

STUART: He was stabbed in the eye.

BRAD: Jesus! Why?

STUART: You'll have to read the book. It's all linked with a
    great labyrinth of intrigue and conjecture.

BRAD: About him being a spy right?

STUART: Yeah. Shakespeare refers to Marlowe's death in As
    You Like It. Touchstone has a line that goes 'something,
    something, something – a great reckoning in a little room'.
    They're pretty sure that's a reference to what happened at
    Deptford.

BRAD: 'A great reckoning in a little room'.

STUART: Yeah.

BRAD: What a wonderful line. 'A great reckoning in a
    little room'. Jesus!

A beat.

STUART: Cath and I have – you know – we've –

BRAD: What? Split?

STUART: Yeah.

BRAD: Oh.

>*A beat.*

>Right. And she called it off? It came from her?

>*STUART nods.*

STUART: Kind of. Then half an hour's silence to kiss it goodbye. Neither of us had anything to say. Weird isn't it? Eight years and –

>*A beat.*

BRAD: Shit. Did you know this was coming?

STUART: Um – um – the truth is – no. No I didn't know it was coming. But then I've always been pretty pathetic about all that.

BRAD: Is there –

STUART: Someone else? Yup.

>*He smiles weakly and shrugs.*

>Tosser.

>*A beat. Then STUART takes his bag and moves towards the door.*

BRAD: What you doing?

STUART: I think I'm – I think I'm going to go Brad.

BRAD: Go? Go where? The tent?

>*A beat. STUART smiles.*

STUART: No. Not the tent. I just think this is all – I don't know – I just think this is all pretty hopeless. I'm not sure there's any point in hanging around here anymore. I –

BRAD: But wait a minute – where you going to go? It's –

STUART: I don't know –

BRAD: – pissing with rain and we're a thousand miles from anywhere! Where you going to go?

STUART shrugs.

STUART: Somewhere. I'll be ok.

STUART moves to the door.

BRAD: Stuart wait a minute. This is stupid! What about the scene?

STUART: What about it?

BRAD: The car's on its way!

STUART: So what?

BRAD: Well –

STUART: What are you going to say? Well when Emilio gets here just say Stuart's gone away. And when you get up the mountain – if you get up the mountain 'cos remember it's Emilio driving – give my best to Derek and the others and just explain that Stuart's truly sorry for any inconvenience but he doesn't want to be part of this film anymore. Ok? I'll tell you something Brad. I really sickened myself today. I –

BRAD: Oh come on you –

STUART: No not drinking! I've done that before and I'll do it again. You know what really sickened me? Rewriting our scene.

BRAD stares at him.

I don't know why I did that.

BRAD: What are you talking about?

STUART: I just don't seem to learn.

BRAD: I don't understand. You came up with some ideas that's all – you –

STUART: It's this horrible desire, this need to make it better, to be constructive – to help out – to – I mean how could I make it better?

BRAD: You tried! What's wrong with –

STUART: Yeah I tried! That's it! I tried! But I failed! And the scene will fail and the film will fail because it's fucking doomed. We know that.

BRAD: This is bullshit!

STUART: It's like drowning men changing their trunks!

A beat.

It fills me with contempt.

BRAD: Who for?

STUART: Myself.

BRAD: Oh really? Well you know what they say?

STUART: What?

BRAD: You feel contempt for yourself then you usually feel it for everyone else as well?

STUART: Who says that?

BRAD: I don't know but it's probably true.

STUART: I don't think so.

A beat.

I'll see you.

BRAD stares at him.

BRAD: Thanks a lot Stuart. Thanks a bunch.

STUART: Look I'm not going because of you. I'm-

BRAD: No? I just told you something I never told anybody and you choose to go. That's fine Stuart! Have a nice life.

STUART: It's got nothing to do with that. I can't –

BRAD: Sure! It's because you feel contempt at yourself for trying to make a pile of shit smell a bit sweeter – well that's really neat! I feel the same thing. Ok? I feel contempt for you too. Only with me it's not because of that.

A beat.

You're a coward. Ok? You're a self-dramatising coward.

STUART: I'm sorry you see it like that.

BRAD: You're what? You're not sorry for anything except yourself! You know? You think all this stuff and you're full of ideas and you can't stop telling us all what's wrong with everything – but when the chips are down you drift into the rain like some ageing hippy and leave everyone else to pick up the pieces. Good! Go! I'll explain to Derek how you're girlfriend's found someone else and you have a drink problem and your grandma got killed in the Blitz. I'm sure he'll be very understanding. After all he's only been up the mountain since six o'clock this morning. It'll be just what he wants to hear!

STUART: How come you're suddenly so concerned about Derek?

BRAD: How old are you? Six?! It's not just Derek! There are forty, fifty people up that mountain! They've been there all day and they're going to be there all day tomorrow – and the next day and the day after that! You think they care about art or drink or girlfriends? They're wet Stuart! They're wet and they're cold and they didn't get any lunch because the truck got stuck in the mud! They've been trying to get something in the can all day but they can't because it's raining.

Ok? You think because I've been here bitching I don't care? You think because we had a drink and spoke some poetry I'm going to join you and walk out the door? Well I'm not!

STUART: I never asked you to join me.

BRAD: Good because I ain't coming. But go ahead – make your heroic gesture! Make the bid for freedom! I'm sure you'll feel a lot less self-contempt that way.

The walkie-talkie suddenly splutters into life making them both jump. Indecipherable, ear-splitting splutter.

BRAD: You're the one who should be in LA! There's plenty of people there feel just like you.

Indecipherable, ear-splitting splutter. STUART sits down with his hands over his face. BRAD picks up the handset.

BRAD: Yeah Chris!

Indecipherable, ear-splitting splutter.

BRAD: Listen where the fuck is Emilio? What's been happening?

Indecipherable, ear-splitting splutter.

BRAD: Jesus!

BRAD relays Chris's news to STUART.

Emilio hit a landslide on the mountain road and nearly went over the edge.

Indecipherable, ear-splitting splutter.

They've had to use a welding torch to cut him out. But he's ok.

Indecipherable, ear-splitting splutter.

And they've what? They've given him another car?! They must be insane!

Indecipherable, ear-splitting splutter.

Yeah – we're ok. Well – kind of. Listen, Stuart wants to tell you something.

BRAD holds the handset out to STUART. There is a beat before STUART takes it. Then he just stands holding it. Indecipherable, ear-splitting splutter. STUART comes to a decision:

STUART: Hi Chris – I just wanted to – I just wanted to –

A beat.

I just wanted to know if – if it's still raining up there?

BRAD smiles. Indecipherable, ear-splitting splutter. STUART relays Chris's weather report to BRAD.

Looks like we're going to get wet.

STUART hangs up.

Jesus! Look at us! Look at the state of us!

STUART goes to the mirror. BRAD stands behind him and they try to do something about their appearance. STUART steps back, looks at BRAD and smiles.

STUART: You know something?

BRAD: What?

STUART: It's weird but – suddenly you look like a conquistador!

BRAD looks at himself in the mirror.

BRAD: You're right. Jesus! Poor bastards!

BRAD looks at STUART.

You too.

A beat.

But the thing is – the thing is Stuart – do you feel like one?

STUART: I dunno.

A beat. STUART thinks.

Maybe a very small one – yeah.

BRAD smiles. He straightens STUART's shirt. STUART adjusts BRAD's jerkin. The rain beats on the roof. Lights fade to black.

THE END

WWW.OBERONBOOKS.COM

 Follow us on www.twitter.com/@oberonbooks
& www.facebook.com/oberonbook

9 781840 029963